LANDMARK COLLECTOR'S LIBR.

THE SPIRIT OF MACCLESFIELD

The 20th Century in Photographs

Doug Pickford

Dedication

This book is dedicated to three wonderful grandchildren: Joseph John Leese, Thomas Douglas Pickford and Zoe Shannon Faith Pickford.

Acknowledgements

This book could not have been compiled and written were it not for the great assistance of my wife Hilary and my mentor, Macclesfield's 'Waterloo Boy' Geoffrey Hunter.

In addition, I would like to thank the following people for their kindness. Many have loaned photographs, others have given of their knowledge of Macclesfield. I am certain to have omitted someone and that error is mine and mine alone. For my forgetfulness I am deeply ashamed and for the unrecorded help of the anonymous I am deeply grateful. Regretfully, some of those mentioned here have now passed away.

Mrs U. Arden, Winifred Armes, Mrs. Arrowsmith, Barbara Bailey, Cliff Bailey, Miss Bailey, Charlie Berisford, Ray Berrisford, Mrs W. P. Blench, Ray Booth, S. Broadhurst, Mrs. Brough, Jack Burgess, Mrs M. Burgess, Rona Cooper, Mike Corcoran, Claire Gosbie, Irene Cross, Barbara Davies, Cyril Dawson, Philip Foster, J. Gorton, Eric Gosling, Norman Gosling, Granelli family, Graham Hackney, Mrs. Hackney, Cherry Ann Hamm, Hancox family, Denis Heapy, Shelagh Hill, Mr and Mrs Michael Holland, Sheila Holland, Mr and Mrs Holland, Mrs Hilda Jones, Mr D. Kendrick, Arthur Kent, Jack Kershaw, Les Kirkham, Margaret Lockett, V. Lomas, Joyce MacDonald, Muriel Massey, Miss G. Matthews, Joan Mottershead, Owen Mulrooney, T. Nolan, P. Nevitt, Muriel Oakes, John Patterson, Mrs M. Penn, Mrs Thelma Perkins, Margaret Pickford, Geoffrey Pownall, Mrs Kathleen Pye, D.B. Read, Peter Robinson, Myra Ross, Mrs Shaw, Eric Sherratt, Colin Shingles, Joyce Shufflebotham, K. Simpson, Philip Smith, Eric Stevenson, Dave Swanson, Don Warren, Doug Warren, John Warren, the Warren family, Martin Welch, Doreen Whittaker, John Williams, Maurice Winnell, Mrs Doris Wolstenholme, Mr J. Wood.

Across: The old fountain in Park Green

THE SPIRIT OF
MACCLESFIELD

THE 20TH CENTURY IN PHOTOGRAPHS

Doug Pickford

Published by

Landmark Publishing Ltd,

Ashbourne Hall, Ashbourne, Derbyshire DE6 1EJ, England
Tel: (01335) 347349 Fax: (01335) 347303
e-mail: landmark@clara.net www.landmarkpublishing.co.uk

1st edition

ISBN 1 84306 008 6

British Library Cataloguing in Publication Data: a catalogue record for this book is
available from the British Library.

Printed by CPI Bath
Designed by Ashley J. Emery
Cover by James Allsopp

Front cover: Three magnificent shire horses at Gurnett Smithy, Sutton.
The Old King's Head is to the left.
Back cover Top: HRH Prince Henry the Duke of Gloucester arrives at
Macclesfield Town Hall, 1929
Back cover Middle: The top of Jordangate and Beech Lane, 1920s
Back cover Bottom: A school outing from Sutton, 1948

Contents

Foreword

By Geoffrey Hunter
(author of *'Waterloo Boy'*)

I am flattered that Doug Pickford has asked me to introduce this book to its readers. Prior to my retirement in 1992 Doug and I had never met but in the years since we have become very good friends indeed. As editor of the Macclesfield Express and since his departure from that post, Doug and his wife Hilary – who is a magazine editor in her own right – have given me much gentle, good-humoured encouragement to enhance my twilight years as a literary dabbler, and I am more grateful than I can say.

I give them my fullest support in their quest to safeguard, for posterity, any item relating to Macclesfield's past, particularly photographs, documents and memories, and to display them in a succession of books.

This latest photographic record, the fourth of this type Doug has produced, combines the opportunism of the professional, the amateur and the novice photographer to stop time in its tracks; to enable us to compare what we once had with what we have today.

Naturally, on a personal note, I enjoy being reminded of the thirties years of my childhood. Times were not easy and most families struggled to survive from one Friday pay-day to the next, but I recall the constancy, and the warm cohesive friendliness and trust of the more gracious age.

'Spirit of Macclesfield' brings Doug's total book publications, embracing our area of Cheshire and neighbouring Derbyshire and Staffordshire, to a grand total of thirteen.

Lucky for some? Not a bit of it! I commend this book to ALL.

Although by then in her 70s, Geoffrey Hunter's mother, Annie, was still working at Brocklehurst Whiston's Hurdsfield Mill in the 1950s. She is pictured in this group. Back row, left to right: 1, Mrs Ball; 3 Ethel Garside; 5 Annie Hunter; 6 Edna Gee; 7 Betty Hudson; 8 Daisy Morris. Left, front row: Albert Smith.

This book was not my idea. I had, as some people may know, already produced half a dozen publications on Old Macclesfield, three of them pictorial, and it was not my intention to (in my eyes at least) over-egg the pudding. But I had not reckoned on a great number of Maxonians who constantly asked, and indeed implored, when I was to produce another book on this great town. And I had not reckoned on Lindsey Porter of Landmark Publishing. When we first met, Lindsey was very matter of fact and businesslike. He thought it a good idea if a quality publication was produced on Macclesfield and I was the person to do it. I was flattered but part of me said No. Another part said YES, YES YES! Little did he or I realise at the time, but we had known each other in early childhood from whence our paths took different twists and turns only to join together as twin chroniclers of the past. He soon persuaded me that this *Spirit of Macclesfield* was a book which needed to be compiled, and when I saw just what he had done with a similar publication on Ashbourne, creating a first-class piece of work with which people of that Derbyshire town were delighted, my mind was made up. Macclesfield was worthy of quality and that is what it should have.

One of the reasons I was slightly negative about the prospects of another book was that I had already used hundreds upon hundreds of photographs in previous publications, and I was not certain there would be sufficient in quantity and quality to allow such a major undertaking, but a trawl through my cupboards, drawers and brown paper boxes showed otherwise. In addition, I have been helping to produce a magazine entitled Old Macc, along with my wife Hilary, and readers of that quarterly publication have been extremely kind in searching through family albums, family trees and family records to bring forward countless priceless photographs for Maxonians all over the world to share. It is all these good people I have to thank, and many individuals as well. Some pictures may have been on public view before, but they all combine to show the true spirit of this wonderful town. Please accept this selection as showing what the book says: the *spirit* of the town.

I have said it before and I will say it again that Macclesfield is unique and so are its inhabitants. Today, the former Silk Town nestling under the East Cheshire hills by the meandering River Bollin, is a Boom Town. When I was the editor of its local weekly newspaper, the Macclesfield Express I watched it grow and grow and grow. Unfortunately, I also saw it change.

The town had come into the twentieth century riding on the crest of a wave. Victoria still reigned and Macclesfield silk was like the British Empire: proud, matchless, incomparable. Its workers numbered many thousands and the silk barons were, in the main, people to be looked up to. Of course there had been the odd rotten apple in the barrel but, in the main, Mester Brocklehurst, Mester Smale, Mester Frost and all the other Mesters were indeed worthy of respect. They were the major employers of the town and the major employees were female. Macclesfield was not only a Silk Town it was a Women's Town. It was they who, in the main, brought home the bacon; it was they who were the skilled workers. True, men were also employed in the mills but it was the lasses the industry could not do without. It was they who had the nimble fingers, it was they who had the deftness, it was they who made Macclesfield Silk a world leader.

But it was the men who went off to fight World War I. It was the sons and cousins, uncles and fathers who marched from The Barracks to join the Cheshires, it was the women who wept.

Those who returned found the old town pretty similar to when they had left. Silk still ruled and the Silkmen were still on th'Moss when Saturday came.

Between the wars, the Carnival was a chance to have a good time. It was a chance to weigh up the mill girls as they vied for the honour of being Silk Queen of Great Britain, it was a time to meet friends and neighbours after the parade in South Park. It was also a time of the Silver Screen. Much courting was done on the back row of the Majestic Cinema, even more at the Drome, not forgetting the Bug Hut (The Regal), The Cinema on Buxton Road and The Premier. At Easter, lovers young and old could walk to Tytherington and along Bluebell Lane, or to Henbury and Bluebell Woods. There wasn't much traffic about then; Syd Gleave could be seen up and down on his special motor bikes, Old Man Simister was always good for a new Austin or something similar, and on really warm summer days it was possible to stroll to Siddington and back without meeting a motor car. A picnic along the Bollin at Prestbury was something to look forward to. There were a number of 'posh' houses there then, but it was still a quaint village, not the large sprawl we have today.

Then came Hitler's War. Again the lads marched off, but a little more apprehensively this time. We had seen the consequences of the previous fight against Germany, and the women wept again.

While the lads were away, it was up to the ladies to do their bit. The mills and factories turned their attention to winning the war. Our airmen wore silk parachutes, safe and sound for having been made here in Macc. Khaki uniforms were turned out by the countless thousands and the mill girls even turned their hands to making strands of aluminium to be dropped to confuse the enemy's radar systems. Yes, there is no doubt about it: Macclesfield helped the war effort far more than the majority of towns.

And those who returned found the old town was still pretty much the same. Jean Alexander, who many will recall as *Coronation Street's* Hilda Ogden, and others will remember as *The Last of the Summer Wine's* Aunty Wainwright came to Macclesfield shortly after the war to act with the Adelphi Players. These were a motley crew who had come together after initially entertaining the thousands of Londoners in the underground stations during the Blitz. Anyway, Jean once told me: 'Macclesfield was a cosy town in those days. Everyone was so friendly, they really made me feel at home and made me welcome. They were lovely people and the town was like a big woollen blanket. It wrapped itself around you.' Some years later, in the early 1970s, she returned and was horrified by what she saw.

She explained: 'They (meaning the planners on the council) had ruined it. They had devastated it; they had knocked places down, they had tried to build new roads, it was hardly recognisable as the Macclesfield I once knew. I could have cried.'

She wasn't alone. So many bemoan the changing face of the place they hold so dear. If only the clock could be turned back!

The big alterations began in the 1950s. First of all, man made fibres came onto the scene and some of the mills tried to move with the times. Cheslyne and Crepes on London Road, for instance, experimented with the new Nylon and Rayon and the crimping process that resulted in the icon of 1960s' fashion, Crimplene, was invented there by Mario Nava. The machine makers Ernest Scragg and Sons stopped making machines to produce silk and began to set their sights on those for the New Nylon Age. And as this progression from silk to man-made materials was creeping upon us, along came the Hurdsfield Industrial Estate – and changed Macclesfield beyond recognition. All of a sudden there was that vast conglomerate ICI and the immensely rich Geigy Pharmaceuticals in town. The then town clerk, Walter Isaac, was to the fore in bringing these industries here, despite the attempts by the silk barons to keep them at bay. The mill owners knew only too well what would happen if these huge firms came to town, and they were proved right. The highly skilled workers found they could earn more money by leaving their staple trade behind and moving to the ultra-modern factories at Hurdsfield away from the old-fashioned silk mills. It was the death knell for the industry, but a life line for Macc.

Supermarkets began to sprout up – the first was Cooper's, later Fine Fare in Mill Street – and the cinemas began to close. The Cinema shut its doors, to be followed by the Premier. The Bug Hut hung on for dear life but became a night club and casino. It was down to the Drome (the Picturedrome) and the Majestic, but eventually the Drome succumbed and became a bingo hall. The Majestic stood firm until the mid 1990s and now that great age of 'The Flicks' has faded into history, like Macclesfield silk.

The 1960s was a time when anything and everything old had to be discarded and the 'contemporary' and modern was 'in'. The mop-topped Beatles played at the El Rio (now a supermarket) in Queen Victoria Street and during the interval walked across the road to 'The Cav' (The Cavendish Coffee Bar) and ordered egg and bacon butties. They were served by a young girl named Hilary who is now my wife.

An area of the town around Victoria Park which comprised many hundreds of terraced homes was demolished in the name of progress and the entire community, some whose families had been there for three or four generations, were moved. A monstrous concrete carbuncle was erected in its place and became known as Victoria Park Flats. I won't tell you what quite a number of people in town called them. Anyway, these are now making way for more new housing – just over 30 years since they were built. What a sad and sorry waste they proved to be.

If only Rod Hackney the 'royal' architect had been on the scene some few years earlier, perhaps it would all have been different. Mr Hackney came to town as a young architect and was living in Black Road. The corporation wanted to do the same with the Black Road area as had been done to the Victoria Park homes, but Rod would have none of it. He organised the residents and persuaded the council that rather than demolish these houses, they should be renovated. The Black Road Community Action development became the blueprint for many other schemes up and down the land and countless communities have since been saved. The fame of Black Road reached the ears of Prince Charles who came along to see for himself.

Much more happened to Macclesfield in the latter decades of the twentieth century and, unfortunately, it was not all for the best. It is no wonder, then, that countless Maxonians choose not to leave the past, but to remember with great affection their younger days in good old Treacle Town.

Yes, those indeed were the days. The days of Smiths Ales, the Angel Hotel, holidays at Barnaby, frosty mornings and crackling fires, steam trains and North Western buses, Yok Salt who sold salt from a block from house to house, Rosie the tramp who would often sleep in the outside privies, Tripe Joe from Jordangate, the UCP in Chestergate and tongue-burning hot chips from Greens in Mill Street, dances at the Stanley Hall. The Hole i'th' Wall and plenty more. Each and every reader will have different memories.

I have endeavoured to include a cross-section of photographs that show Macclesfield in its many guises. I have included a number of school class photos because I feel they show not only the people of the town but how society has changed over the years. The individuals I have included and mentioned are not meant to be my idea of the epitome of Old Macc, they are but a cross-section of Maxonians, and no slight is intended on anyone whom I have not included.

I have endeavoured to acknowledge as many people as possible who have supplied photographs but I, inevitably, have omitted some. This has been done for no other reason than the fact that I am becoming forgetful. My sincere apologies to anyone I have not included.

And last but not least, I must make mention of two people. Number one: Hilary, my wife, whose encouragement, assistance and love I appreciate greatly and Number Two: Geoffrey Hunter, a Maxonian through and through, whose love of the town, whose knowledge and affection of Macclesfield I have found to be of immeasurable assistance. This book could not have been produced without them and without countless other true blue Maxonians.

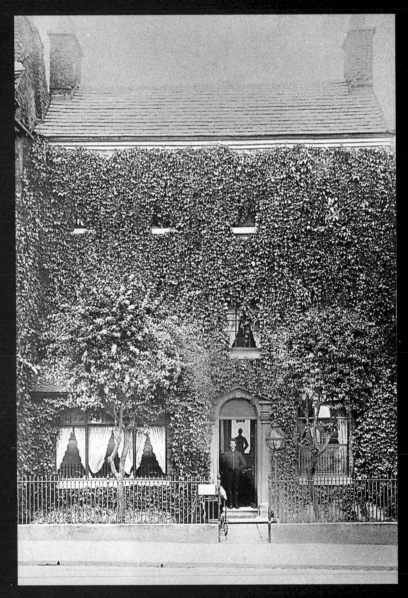

Older residents may recall Mr. Bates the dentist's house and surgery in Park Green. This ivy-covered building was formerly owned by the Pickford family and was known as Pickford Eyes Farm in the years before the eighteenth century. The farm land extended east, hence Pickford Street today.

Looking up from Park Green to Park Street, leading to Park Lane. Dr Somerville's residence, another ivy-clad building, is on the left. It was later to become the registry office and is now private offices. Notice the two carters in the middle of the road at the top, pausing for a chat.

    This postcard is postmarked April 29, 1905, but the view may have been taken some seven or eight years before that date.

The view to what is now Park Green Memorial Gardens but was then still a green space where horse fairs were held. Further up the road around Cross Street was the scene of another market for many centuries, and it is thought there was a market cross there, hence the street's name.

Mr Bates's dental surgery is to the right, adjacent to the London and Manchester Railway parcels office, next door to which was (around 1910) a pawnbroker's. The sign of the three balls can be seen by the drain spout if you look closely.

The Congregational Church, now United Reformed Church, with Depot Mill in the background. To the churches right is the bank building now occupied by Barclays. This photograph was taken around the year 1920.

This celebration of the Spirit of Macclesfield cannot let Macclesfield's glorious piece of Victorian whimsy go unrecorded. The fountain in Park Green, outside the old library buildings, was a delight. Unfortunately it fell victim to the 'War Effort' in World War II and was taken down.

Early Edwardian Maxonians pose for the photographer around the fountain (save for the nonchalant young chap on the left, it appears).

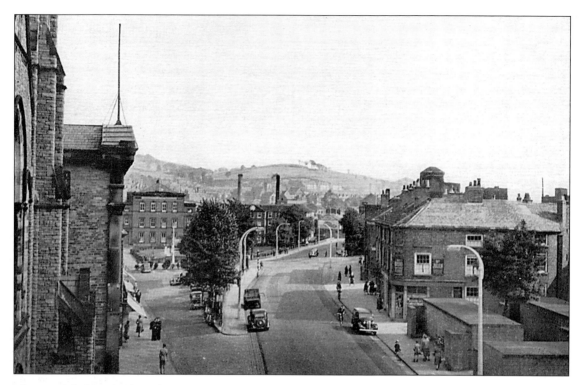

The intrepid photographer of this fine view southwards must have climbed to the top of the Congregational Church tower for this early 1950s view of Park Green.

More down to earth: Macclesfield Equitable Provident Society's premises were in full swing when this shot was taken a few years after the World War II. Does anyone recall Morris's stores (pictured behind the car drawing up to the traffic lights)?

The Market Place was, for countless centuries, the hub of the town. In the 1980s there was still a market, of sorts, by the side of the town hall where the new civic offices are now situated. It was still called Union Gateway, although the gateway to the Union pub had gone many years previously. That fish van was there for a good many years.

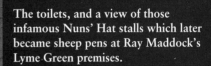

The toilets, and a view of those infamous Nuns' Hat stalls which later became sheep pens at Ray Maddock's Lyme Green premises.

Another view of the market in the 1980s.

The old Guild Hall in the Market Place from an old print in 1823. This was the year the building was demolished and it is therefore surmised that this is why the drawing was produced. The Town Hall we know now was built 1823-4 from a design by architect Frances Goodwin. A new frontage was added between 1869-71. The railings at the front of the Guild Hall were where felons and other offenders were once tied before they were flogged. An old Macc saying was: 'You'll have me tied to th' Guild Hall steps' meaning 'You will get me into trouble'.

Rather worn with age but nevertheless evocative of the 1930s when the market stalls were a permanent fixture. Note the Westminster Bank (left) and Boots Chemists on the opposite side of Chestergate's entrance.

Leach & Sons chemists, Timpson's shoe shop and a policeman on point duty are features of this late 1950s view of the Market Place towards Mill Street.

Turning the camera northwards towards the District Bank, now the library buildings.

The Parish Church of St Michael and All Angels in all its glory, with a few market stalls outside. Just why there should have been a dearth of traders is not clear.

A busy Market Place scene. This is how the market really was: a bustling and vibrant hub of Old Macclesfield.

During the early or perhaps mid 1960s, the scene was very much the same. Don't forget that the road down to Mill Street and beyond from Jordangate, passing the front of the Town Hall, was the major trunk route from Manchester to Derby.

A North Western Road Car Company bus turns down Chestergate and cars are parked outside the old Angel Hotel (demolished 1969).

A vintage car, believed to have been owned by Lt Col Philip Brocklehurst, Bart, of Swythamley Hall, is parked outside the Town Hall. Of course, that machine was a modern motor at this time. In the background, a horse and cart trots towards it.

A view from the Market Place down Chestergate. Parr's Bank, later the Natwest, is on the left. Just by Miss Brocklehurst's landau on the right was Pott and Thompson's much renowned store later in the century. That freshly ground coffee smell still lingers in some memories.

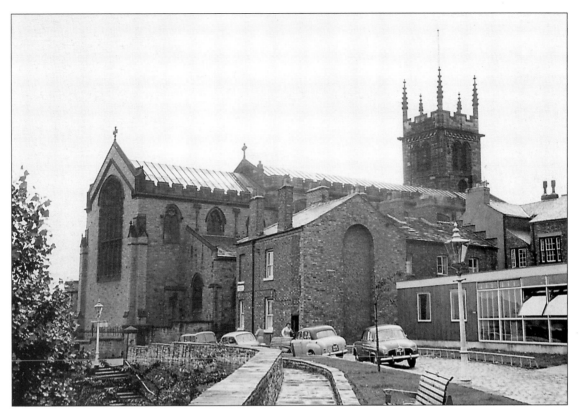

Behind the Market Place was, up until the 1960s/70s the Council Housing Offices (right).

And of course, still in situ today, the Civic Gardens or Step Hill Gardens which some refer to as Sparrow Park.

Chapter 3 - The Waters

Waters Green, Macclesfield, from Albert Place. Lomas's Mill is on the left, then Cookson's Central Garage. The Old Millstone and the Bull and Gate are prominent and, to the left, the well-known 'Jacob's Ladder' footpath to Churchside can be seen. Note, also the 'Bottom Market' stalls.

A view from Central Station with the Nag's Head to the right. The Bull and Gate and Nag's Head names denote the horse and cattle fairs and markets held there whilst the Old Millstone is testament to the King's Bakehouse and corn mill which was by the River Bollin in medieval days. The Waters, or Waters Green, is named after the river running through the valley, of course.

Brunswick Hill, from The Waters to the back of the Parish Church.

The sign is advertising Bagshaw & Turner's estate agents as the road wends up to Church Wallgate from The Waters in this 1970s photograph.

The entrance to Church Wallgate during the 1970s. Prout's tobacconists, a feature for many years, is to the right, behind the chap washing his sports car. Perhaps the picture was taken on a Sunday.

An evocative picture of Brunswick Hill, looking down to The Waters. What was the errand lad carrying in the basket, I wonder?

Kirk's restaurant, dining and tea rooms to the right of the Nag's Head, with the 108 Steps leading up to the Parish Church. This was probably taken about 1910.

A fine shot taken from the bottom of Chestergate, the road to Chester, showing the lower half of that main street. Pitts Hardware is shown on the site upon which The Picturedrome was later built. The Dispatch poster outside the newsagent's declaring 'Natal's Reply to Allegations of Barbarity' indicates Second Boer War conflict and a date between 1899 and 1902.

The top end of Chestergate looking to the Town Hall in the early 1900s.

Mill Street from a point where McDonald's restaurant is now situated (right) looking north to the Market Place, with Stanley Street top left, now the entrance to the Grosvenor Centre.

Seymour Mead and Burgons' grocers on the right half way down Mill Street, looking southwards. The white tower of The Majestic cinema can be seen in the background.

Looking up Mill Street in this late 1920s shot, from outside the White Lion public house. The photo is somewhat scratched because of the fact that the glass plate from which it was taken, was found in the drawer of an old sideboard at a house in James Street.

A late 1960s view from Mill Street down Pickford Street. All these buildings to the left have now gone. This was taken before the Co-op superstore was built at the bottom left of the picture.

These extremely old buildings cornering on to Pinfold Street (where stray farm and domestic animals used to be kept before the nineteenth century) from the bottom of Chester Road. Sheldon's butchers (left) was there in the 1970s when this shot was taken.

Jordangate, looking to Hibel Road and Beech Lane, in the early part of the twentieth century.
    The Rifleman Inn can be seen in all its glory. Those delightful houses are still there, I am pleased to say. Part of the buildings in the background housed Bullock Bros, the photographers, before becoming a chemist's.

Duke Street, from the corner of Charles Street ('Mr Hardern's Mill') to Duke Street School, 1957.

This mid to late 1960s bird's eye view of The Navigation Inn, Black Road, in the foreground before demolition took place in Black Road itself, plus Windmill Street, Copper Street and Gunco Lane. Factory chimneys seen in the top right hand quarter of the photograph, i.e., Copper Street Dye Works, A.B. Carlisle's, Backhouse and Coppock, Soho Mill, London Road Mill, and White's Dyehouse, High Street, are no longer in existence today.

This photograph of Hurdsfield Road and its junction with Mason's Lane is probably Edwardian in vintage. Today The Flower Pot occupies the corner on the left. The original Flower Pot Inn can be seen a few yards further up the road.

The Old Royal Oak Hotel casts a mid-morning shadow in this 1930 photograph taken from a bedroom window at 41 Buxton Road by teenager Frank Burgess. His father had the butcher's shop and his mother the greengrocer's shop on the short hill above the newsagent's premises of Mr G.W. Billington.

Brocklehurst Whiston's Mill, Hurdsfield. The Crescent, Brocklehurst Avenue and Queen's Avenue are shown.

This is a very old photograph of Waters Green and surrounding area taken from a point behind Macclesfield's new Town Hall at the extreme left of the Hawthorn Street Garden Walk. The brief glimpse of road in the foreground is leading to Buxton Road railway bridge. In those days it is clear that both sides of the road were built upon as it approached Gas Road. Although the railway can be seen the congestion of property in the middle distance which was substantially cleared to make way for the Central Railway Station in 1872 would seem to date this pre-1870.

A photograph of Commercial Road believed to have been taken in 1908. The photographer's tripod was stood on the pavement outside The Woodman Inn.

Sunderland Street, Macclesfield, looking to Central Station.

The corner of Windmill Street and Calamine Street in the early 1960s.

The top end of Park Lane looking to the town centre.

Broken Cross from Pexhill Road about 1900-1905.

Oxford Road, with the former Oxford Road Hotel on the right. Dunkerley's Mill can be seen in the background.

'I will lift up mine eyes unto the hills. . . .' Hurdsfield Road in the 1920s.

Goodall Street in the late 1950s, possibly early 1960s, from Bond Street.

Castle Street, Derby Street and Great King Street are shown in this aerial photograph prior to the construction of Churchill Way.

The street running from centre top to centre left is Great King Street. The old building top left is the former Christ Church School before demolition.

A leafy Oxford Road in more placid days. It is believed this house was Fermain, later to be the site of the Boys' Club, but this is not confirmed.

An employee of the North Stafford Railway, which came through Macclesfield (right) looks at the cameraman, along with two boys, in Bond Street. The lad in the middle is carrying suitcases and may have had something to do with the railway man.

The old Co-op building at the corner of Sunderland Street and Park Green is proudly standing in the background. Even prouder stands the war memorial, immortalising those local folk who gave their lives in the conflicts. We shall always remember them.

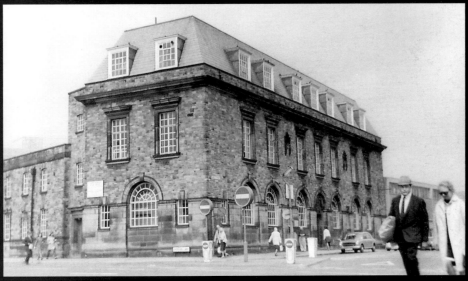

Local masons chiselled out the Kerridge stone to build the town's new post office in Castle Street during the early part of the 1920s. Later the magnificent building became the headquarters for the Cheshire Building Society. In this early 1970s picture, Churchill Way had just been built and the post office was still in situ.

Now demolished: the side of number 17 Waterloo Street and the fronts of numbers 2,4,6 and 8 Daybrook Street.

A back yard in Daybrook Street where the house fronts faced Victoria Park (see tree branches behind chimneys).

Another street now gone: Queen Street. The shop used to be the steam bakery, a very popular establishment that sold their own cakes and cream scones, plus special fruit pies.

The Dumber, a piece of land looking to the Alms Houses on Buxton Road, showing Clark's shop on the corner of Waterloo Street/Davies Street (on The Dumber). At the time of this photograph, around 1967 just prior to demolition, this was a house but was formerly a shop. The photo is taken from outside the Selling Out shop which used to be Ripley's off licence.

The bottom of Waterloo Street, with the photographer's back to Commercial Road. Challinor's mill can be seen.

A rather unusual photo taken in October, 1958, of the rear of the shop and house in Bank Street.

R. Marshall Carr Ltd's electrical shop in Mill Street, formerly the Pig and Whistle pub. This name probably derived from 'The Pagan Wassail'. Notice the chewing gum machine on the side of the shop (left) offering YZ Gum for 1d and the chocolate machine offering a bar of Terry's chocolate for 3d.

Remember the corporation gas works in (where else but) Gas Road? The sign on the side proclaims 'Use Gas'. This was manufactured on the premises as it were and stored in the gasometer at the bottom of Hurdsfield.

A fine study of the 1502-built building believed to have been part of the old grammar school sited behind St Michael's Church. Sparrow Park now occupies this area.

A view of Macclesfield Infirmary over 90 years ago. It was demolished in the early 1990s to make way for a supermarket.

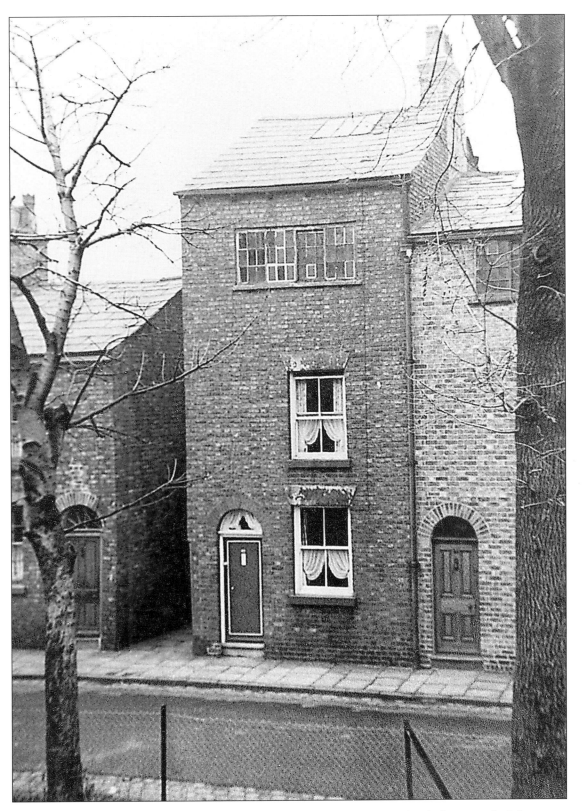

Taken from Victoria Park looking at Daybrook Street. The school was to the left. The house on the left was Kirkham's for many years.

The old Sunday School in Roe Street, later the Silk Heritage Centre. To the left at the time of this photograph, approximately 1910, was Brook's slate and pipe yard.

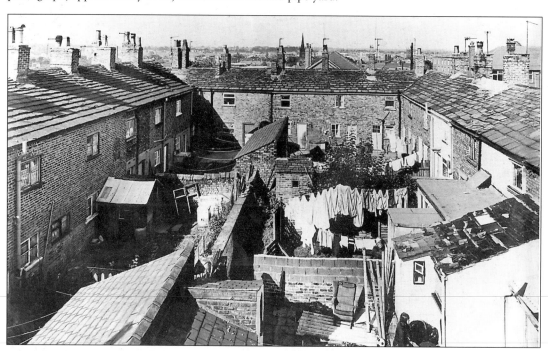

In the early 1970s, architect Rod Hackney, later to be an adviser to Prince Charles, spearheaded the Black Road Action Group which campaigned for the residents' homes to be saved from demolition and the residents would all chip in to improve each other's homes. The old Macclesfield Borough Council agreed, and these homes, part of the second Black Road scheme, were saved. They are pictured before work commenced.

The official opening of KEK Ltd. on Hurdsfield Industrial Estate during the 1960s. Mr. Roy Cooper shows the Town Clerk, Mr. Walter Isaac, machinery manufactured by the company. At the back are Mr. Tom Platt (Chief Engineer), Mr. Norman Gosling (Company Secretary/Accountant) and a Swiss representative.

Macclesfield's MP Air Commodore Sir Arthur Vere Harvey is greeted by Managing Director Mr Roy Cooper at the official opening of KEK Ltd on Hurdsfield.

A photograph taken in the canteen at Hewetson's, London Road, Macclesfield. The occasion was obviously a special one.

An aerial view of Frost's Mill, for so many years one of the principal employers in the Macclesfield area. At one time the power for the looms and other machines came from a water wheel, the casing for which can be seen in this 1920s picture, to the right, along Mill Lane.

The building to the left was Park Green Methodist Chapel, used as a British Canteen during the World War II. The chapel closed shortly after the war. The cenotaph can be seen at the bottom of the picture.

Taken about 1949, this shows the ladies of Vernons. I understand that Vernon's premises were in Henderson Street or thereabouts.

Bond Street Manufacturing Co., early in the twentieth century. Forelady Mrs Nellie Byrne is seen in the background, left. Her uncle Albert Byrne was the owner or the manager. The company started at the turn of the century and ceased in the 1970s. They were manufacturers of silk neckwear for ladies.

A shot taken probably in the 1930s at John Abraham and Bros Ltd's piece dye house.

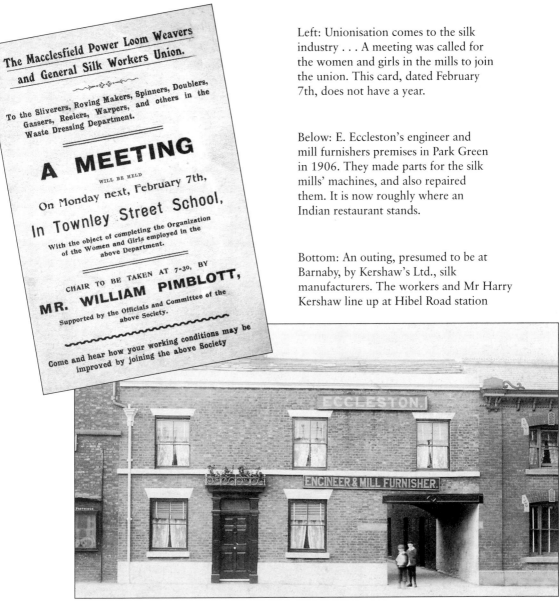

The Macclesfield Power Loom Weavers and General Silk Workers Union.

To the Sliverers, Roving Makers, Spinners, Doublers, Gassers, Reelers, Warpers, and others in the Waste Dressing Department.

A MEETING

WILL BE HELD

On Monday next, February 7th,

In Townley Street School,

With the object of completing the Organization of the Women and Girls employed in the above Department.

CHAIR TO BE TAKEN AT 7-30, BY

MR. WILLIAM PIMBLOTT,

Supported by the Officials and Committee of the above Society.

Come and hear how your working conditions may be improved by joining the above Society

Left: Unionisation comes to the silk industry . . . A meeting was called for the women and girls in the mills to join the union. This card, dated February 7th, does not have a year.

Below: E. Eccleston's engineer and mill furnishers premises in Park Green in 1906. They made parts for the silk mills' machines, and also repaired them. It is now roughly where an Indian restaurant stands.

Bottom: An outing, presumed to be at Barnaby, by Kershaw's Ltd., silk manufacturers. The workers and Mr Harry Kershaw line up at Hibel Road station

Mr W.R. Wadsworth, Managing Director of Frost's Park Green Mill. The date is not known but is probably the 1930s.

The General Office at William Frost's Park Green Mill.

This photograph was taken at Brocklehurst Whiston's Hurdsfield Mill before the World War II.

Taken in 1947 this commemorates presentations to Hovis employees. The lady is Mrs Lillian Hodkinson, then of 18 Brook Street, Macclesfield and the gentleman making the presentations is Mr John F. Morton.

Silk dressers at Hurdsfield Mills (Brocklehurst Whiston). Top row: J. F. Gee (56 and a half years' service), then two others with the same long-serving record: F. Potts and E. Parker; R. Wheelkton (54 and a half), S. Shaw (19), F. Boston (56), J. Brickhill (58 and a half). Front row: H. Clarke (62 and a half), W. Chappell (57 and a half), W. Spooner (67), W. Hulby (47), F. Gregory (foreman, 63), W. Barnett (63), A. Yearsley (51), A. Tomkinson (52), H. Wall (57 and a half), G. Harding (22). The picture was taken some time in the 1930s.

Brocklehurst Whiston's trip to London. Macclesfield people are pictured outside the Houses of Parliament. They had travelled to the city by train and were picked up by charabanc.

Sydney Scragg's 50th birthday party in 1942. Scraggs were machinery manufacturers. Among those identified are: N. Tyler, R. Birch, S. Gorton, L. Barratt, F. Bailey, G. Hodgson, A. Platt, A. Dobson, K. Allen, S. Snape, L. Bancroft, Mr Beard, J. Gill, M. Crawford, M. Bennett, G. Dale, M. Snape, W. Armes, M. Connor, T. Whittaker, A. Lanchberry, R. Barber, R. Moores, J. Hockenhull, A. Hockenhull, C. Armes, F. Scragg, S. Scragg, Mr Scragg.

Cameron Shirts, Macclesfield, enjoy a modest celebration at a local venue (was it the Angel Hotel?) Probably about 1948. Back row, left to right: - - , Mrs. Poolford, Joe Poolford. Second row: Wilf King, Emmie Barnes, Kitty King, Annie King, Mabel Hodkinson, Annie Hodkinson. Front row: — , Percy Rathbone, Ewan Cameron, Mr. Waddilove, Moses King.

Macclesfield Times editorial staff about 1930. Left to right: Harold Smith, George Hollinshead, Philip Murray, Mr. E. Tucker.

For many years up until 1969, the town's leading newspaper, the County Express (later Macclesfield Express) was published and printed from Castle Street. Here production manager Ernie Hackney shares a joke with other Macclesfield printers.

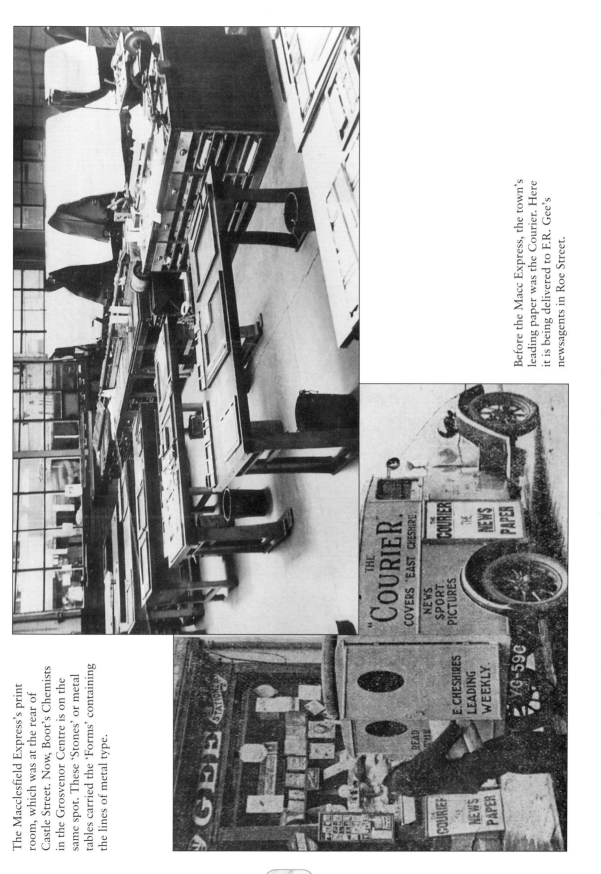

The Macclesfield Express's print room, which was at the rear of Castle Street. Now, Boot's Chemists in the Grosvenor Centre is on the same spot. These 'Stones' or metal tables carried the 'Forms' containing the lines of metal type.

Before the Macc Express, the town's leading paper was the Courier. Here it is being delivered to F.R. Gee's newsagents in Roe Street.

The paper's rotary press running off the Express. The rattle and bangs of the press could be heard in Stanley Street during Wednesday nights.

The end of an era. Editor Clifford Rathbone is presented with a picnic set on the occasion of his retirement in 1972 by Father of the Chapel (union representative) Terry Dean who lived in Station Street. Other names on the photo are Brian Armitt (rear), Bernard Jordan, Jim Statham, Bert Frith and Eric Legh.

One man on a pony and trap trots by the Town Hall in more leisurely times before the internal combustion engine, and when walking was still an accepted occupation.

A late Edwardian photograph. Elijah Burgess, a dealer in goods English and foreign, lived in White Street (with stables at the rear) and in Queen Street at different times and augmented his earnings by delivering items of furniture on his cart for Arighi Bianchi, fastidiously protecting their wares with numerous blankets. Mr Burgess's family are photographed with him.

The canal and canal bridge at Hurdsfield: a picture postcard scene of early in the twentieth century. Notice the block and tackle on the left for loading on to canal barges.

One of Macclesfield's most well-known canal haulage families was the Greens. Here we see Mr and Mrs John Green of Hurdsfield.

Horses and carts are all that can be seen outside the Central Station, in this shot taken around the turn of the century. Notice the cattle pens at the bottom of the picture.

A similar scene but, this time, post World War II. Flat-backed lorries and North Western buses are in evidence.

The camera pans northwards along the line to Buxton Road bridge. The cattle pens for the market can be seen (right).

Again we see Buxton Road bridge and the railway line, but the now demolished area around Commercial Road and Waterloo Street can plainly be seen: a stark reminder of what used to be.

A Manchester to Stoke passenger train waits at Central Station. The later 'improvements' to the station demolished this fine building.

A study in steam. Two fine engines in the Hibel Road engine sheds.

Possibly the last steam passenger train from Macclesfield on 19th June, 1965 to Mold Junction. This Barnaby holiday special 10.08 am Macclesfield to Llandudno is pictured near Sutton, just passing Backouse and Coppocks. The gentleman in the white coat is possibly the landlord of the Railway View, Jock Crawford.

Diesel took over from steam. Here a passenger train waits to go on the Bollington line to London Road station, Manchester, in the 1960s.

A superb photograph taken in the early years of the motor car. The scene is the top of Hibel Road and the delightful car is making its way to Beech Lane. The houses in the background later became Corbishley's garage and then the garage was demolished for the new road. Incidentally, the number plate is EH7. What, I wonder, happened to that? The clarity of this picture, and the fact that it was taken from near to the Beech Lane premises of Bullock Bros photographers points to their being responsible for the historic shot.

Another delightful photograph of a vintage car, this time outside Sycamore Hill, Macclesfield. Geoffrey Hunter informs me the car is similar in style to the Rolls Royce Silver Ghost of 1906, the engine and chassis of which cost £985 with the body cost added. Thanks to Mrs Doreen Powell, we can be informed that a Mrs Stringer lived at Sycamore Hill in 1902. Mr Ron Thornley of Chiltern Avenue has made a suggestion regarding the identity of the gentleman in the car (who may have been visiting at the time). Perhaps he was Mr Gerald Higginbotham, famous for being one of the first people to own a car - and an aeroplane - in Macclesfield. He lived at Ivy Holme close by. He is also remembered for driving his car up the 108 Steps!

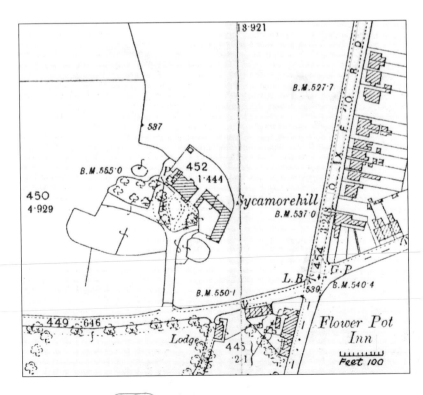

This portion of an 1898 map shows Sycamore Hill as it was at that time.

All ready for the off! An all-male party prepares to leave the Post Office Hotel, Derby Street, for a 1920s outing. The back of the picture says 'E. Cross, fourth from left, seated.' Edward Cross, corn and flour dealer, was at 44 Waters Green.

An early charabanc trip – on a Denis automobile – starting its journey from Park Green, with the old Post Office in the background.

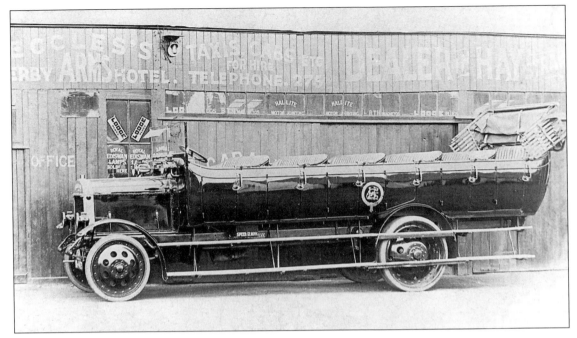

One of the first charabanc owners in Macclesfield was Mr John Etchells at the Derby Arms Hotel in Chestergate, and here is one of his elegant fleet. The photograph was taken in the rear yard of the premises.

The year is 1928 and a car braves the floods in Park Green and along Sunderland Street. I will bet more than a few Macclesfield residents can recall more than one flood at this spot over the years.

Gleave Motors' rescue vehicle outside the showrooms. The now demolished Royal Oak Hotel is in the background.

A lone car drives towards Beech Lane, Tytherington. The fields on the right are now housing and Tytherington High School. Times certainly change.

When Macclesfield's Large Sunday School was in its heyday in Roe Street, children who did not attend their own church Sunday School were obliged to attend the 'communal' one. The Large Sunday School had one person who made sure they did. He was 'affectionately' known as 'The Knobbler' and this is he. It was part of Robert Raikes' pioneering initiative of keeping urchins off the streets. This gentleman, unfortunately his name is not recorded, attended the Sunday School himself as a child.

Left: Harry and Elsie Hancox senr, with Harry jnr. Later Harry jnr and his wife kept the shop and post office at the top of Beech Lane.

Below: Outside 82 High Street, Macclesfield circa 1920. The lady may have been Mrs Johnson.

Harry Hancox jnr in khaki during the World War II. Besides having the Beech Lane shop and post office he and his wife were later landlord and landlady of the Leather's Smithy at Langley.

Right: For many years there was a newsagent's shop in Roe Street near to Mill Street. During the 1930s and onwards the proprietors were Mr and Mrs F. Gee. This lady was a familiar site selling newspapers.

Air Commodore Sir Arthur Vere Harvey, MP for Macclesfield pictured talking to two gentlemen in the late 1940s or early 1950s. He later became Sir Arthur and then Lord Harvey of Prestbury. He was succeeded as Conservative Member of Parliament by Nicholas Winterton.

Above left: Anne Belfield (later Warren) at the rear of her home, 21 Fence Street (the wall on the right is the rear of a house in Welch Street).

Above: Anne Warren in later life in the 1960s at the front of the same house. It has now been demolished.

Left: Mark Warren, then aged about 10 months, in the gutter outside his home, 45 Fence Street, in 1961. Times have certainly changed: it would be a foolish act to allow a baby to do this today, but then traffic was far lighter.

A familiar sight during the 1930s, especially for passengers on the steam trains that chugged along the line to Stoke from Macclesfield was this pigeon loft under the bridge by the side of the River Bollin. The picture shows Harry Bennison of Higginbotham Green displaying his trophies won by the racing pigeons. His son is on the left and his grandson is on the stool. The gent in the middle with the bowler hat was Mr Isaac Cooper.

In 1937 a group of Macclesfield and district people visited Lourdes. Here is Mr Vincent Galgani of Bollington at the holy shrine.

Far left: Edwin Oldfield who was, for 30 years, Macclesfield's official Town Crier. The bell is now in the possession of the Nava family of Macclesfield, now living in Switzerland.

Left: During the 1930s, Broken Cross's police constable and later sergeant was Jim Bowyer, my great uncle.

At the wedding of Mr and Mrs Jack Burgess on March 6th, 1953, pictured in Churchside (notice the snow by the right wall). The wedding guests are Mr and Mrs David Burgess (centre), Amy Burgess (left) and Margaret Burgess, Jack's sister.

The year is 1908 and William and Alice Gardiner with Dora (in arms), Mildred, Lucy and George William (Bill) pose for the camera outside 248/250 Black Road, Macclesfield. The premises are still a shop today.

A picture that typified the houses of Macclesfield: taken at 1 House, 4 Court, Crompton Road (between St Andrew's Road and Crompton Road).

Mrs Edith Alice Storer outside 58 Rainow Road, Hurdsfield, circa 1915. This lady died in 1929 aged 54.

Journalist and fly fisher extraordinaire the late Phillip Murray (left) enjoying a picnic at Tegg's Nose with friends including well-known historian the late Mrs May Carne (second from right).

The apron worn by this lady outside a house in Crompton Road was typical of those worn by countless Maxonian ladies in the 1920s, '30s and '40s. It served both for domestic purposes and for work in the silk mills.

Much could be written (and has been) about the wonderful ice cream that is Granelli's. This should bring back many memories – Mr Granelli in his ice cream cart around the 1930s.

Arthur Smith, well-known fishing tackle purveyor fishing on Macclesfield Canal. Living at 18 Statham Street, he opened a fishing tackle shop at 22 Statham Street. The father of eight, he started his fishing business well before World War II until 1961 when he reluctantly retired aged 69. He was renowned for his handmade rods he constructed himself. People are still using them.

Flooding at Moss Rose before the World War II. The houses had not been built very long.

An Empire Day outing to Little Moreton Hall for teachers, helpers and pupils of St James's School, Sutton Lane Ends, in 1948. The headmaster, Mr Everall, is seen extreme left and Mr Arthur Kent (who supplied this picture) is the young lad wearing the cap on the far right.

An impressive parade at the bottom of Mill Street before World War II. But what was it? The gentlemen with blacked faces in the parade are dressed in tunics with stars on them. Notice the spectators are all wearing hats apart from one gent and a young girl. There is a lady dressed in Chinese costume collecting money (centre left).

Empire Day 1909 and thousands flocked to the Market Place. It was a school holiday but churches and Sunday Schools turned out for the celebrations.

Some very familiar faces at the last meeting of the old Health Committee pictured outside West Park Hospital, the former workhouse.

Macclesfield newsagents and their families got together for an outing to Southport in 1947. They are pictured in Park Green about to get on the omnibus.

It is May 6th 1946, the 150th anniversary of the establishment of the Sunday School in Roe Street and a service is held outside, by the memorial to the founder, John Whittaker.

The Mayor's Sunday Parade marches down Castle Street before turning into Mill Street towards the Parish church. Notice the Farmer's Trading Society offices, Fred Pimblott's and Chester Twemlow's.

A happy Lyme Green gathering celebrating VE Day in 1945.

Victory in Europe celebrations in Armitt Street, Macclesfield. Most of the children are holding Union Jacks – and just look at those wonderful setts in the street.

Yet another street celebration for VE Day – this was in Old Mill Lane.

Old Park Lane with the former library to the left. The occasion is the visit of the Duchess of Teck. Bowler hats appear to have been the order of the day for the gentlemen. The ladies sported bonnets and shawls. The banners proclaim 'Welcome to the Royal Party' and 'Prosperity to the Silk Trade'.

The caption to the photograph says 'Consecration of St Alban's, Macclesfield. October 22, 1931.' It is probably the consecration of Canon Cleary by the Bishop of Shrewsbury.

The beautiful Belgium Black horses drawing youngsters at an event at perhaps Moss Rose or, more likely, in a field behind the Star Inn, London Road, during the 1920s or thereabouts.

Officials and choir of St Peter's Church, Windmill Street, 1950. The occasion was probably the induction of the vicar, John Richards. He left the parish in 1956 to become vicar at New Brighton before completing his ministry at Hoylake. Standing, left to right: J Mudge, —, John Burges, Mavis Hillman, Fred Hillman, Jack Burgess, Mr Hargreaves, Abraham Wood, Albert Williams (warden), H Harpur, Rev Richards, Sid Cox, Harold Varty (warden), Tom Heapy (verger), Harry Smith, Tom Hansell (lay reader), E Whitehurst, Charles Rothwell (organist/choirmaster). Seated: Marian Rothwell, Betty Murphy, Lizzie Hudson, Mary Hillman, Thelma Bailey, Barbara Hayes, Helen Varty, Joan Williams, Mrs Williams, Miss Beck.

St George's Choir in the early 1930s.

Crowds gathered at the bottom of Buxton Road, with the Royal Oak in the background. The gentleman in the white coat centre right is John Alcock, the landlord of the Oxford Road Tavern in Macclesfield, who was commencing his walk – backwards – from Macclesfield to Buxton in 1902, 27 years after his original walk, backwards, to Buxton. This time it took him three hours and 14 minutes.

Staff of Burdin's, Mill Street. Second from the right is George Burdin and fourth from the right is Will Burdin. Far left is Arthur Burdin.

St George's Rose Queen, June 16th 1934. She was C. Watson (was it Christine or Carol?). Attendants were K. Greaves, D. Bennet, G. Alcock and H. Mitchell. The herald was Roy Robinson, crown bearer was Ian Smith. Train bearers: K. Dean, J. Bullock.

'With it' Macclesfield young people at Butlin's Holiday Camp, Phwelli, some time in the early 1950s.

The venue is outside the Stanley Hall in Castle Street and these children in fancy dress have obviously been to a special occasion. The year is probably 1931. Among those posing for the picture are: Mildred Horrocks, Joan Breeze, Joan Booth and her sister, Ken Morbray, Pat Carless, Peggy Heels, Margaret Gledhill. Joan Savage is centre front with the England sash.

This Waters Green scene of 1930 was the setting for the 'coronation' of Macclesfield's (and Britain's) first Silk Queen, Miss Lillian Jervis, who was employed by Madge Dunkerley, Oxford Road Mill. Miss Jervis became Mrs Dale in due course. A lady who, as a little girl, was present at this ceremony recalls the huge crowd at ground level and at windows and remembers a swarm of spectators climbing up the steps – known as Jacob's Ladder – by the side of the Prout brothers' newsagent and tobacconist businesses, to get an elevated view of the proceedings. The Silk Queen proceedings were part of the carnival festivities.

Local ladder-makers J. Fowler and Son, Canal Street, are all ready to join the procession in this 1930s' carnival photograph.

Macclesfield's first-ever Silk Queen Lillian Jervis in South Park during the 1930s carnival and coronation.

A Macclesfield Silk Queen and Silk Princesses in South Park after the carnival parade.

John Green, haulage contractor's, lorry decorated for one of the carnivals during the 1930s. The proceeds of the event went towards the upkeep of the Infirmary.

The 'Marcovitch Cigarette Girls' complete with cigarette holders and top hats walk arm in arm past the old Swan wi' Two Necks in Chestergate during the carnival parade.

Ernest Slack driving a float in Macclesfield Carnival, year unknown, when he was working for Sinnetts – pre-1941 as he commenced a bus driving career in 1941.

This photo of a North Western Road Car Company bus made ready to join the Macclesfield Carnival procession was taken in King Edward Street looking towards Jordangate. I have no names or dates for this picture but is probably an early 1930s pose.

Beefeaters and ladies of Merrie England prepare to join the carnival parade in 1932.

What a picture! A motley crew all dressed up for the carnival fun and games. The men may have been from one of the many grocers' shops in town, perhaps Seymour Meads.

The newly-revived carnival in 1971 included The Acromacs, and this young lady was one of the stars!

The year is 1931 and pupils of Lillian Murphy's Dancing School line up in South Park by the steps in front of the old Pavilion after they had taken part in the parade.

A young policeman and his older prisoner in a
1930s parade.

The Silk Queen is driven up Park Street into
Park Lane.

The Silk Queen and retinue in Chestergate.

'Appy 'Ambone's Piccalli Players from The Dams.

The Hazel Grove Twins: favourites in the pre-war carnivals. Make them laugh and they paid you. If you didn't manage to . . . You paid them. The proceeds went to the Infirmary.

With the King's School in the background, these gents appear to represent law officers through the ages and are pictured on Cumberland Street playing field.

Proudly marching; The Beach Brigade.

J. Albinson of 28 Roe Street, Macclesfield, took this photograph of 'Romans' prior to the carnival.

A. W. Hewetson's London Road Mill Beach and Lido Girls.

The carnival was reintroduced in the 1970s. Public houses dressed their exteriors to be in the carnival spirit, and here MP Nicholas Winterton, Justice of the Peace Pat Baron (President of the Carnival Committee) and Macclesfield Express editor Doug Pickford have the hard task of judging.

The GPO provided this prize-winning float Postman Through the Ages in 1971.

Macclesfield Banjo, Mandolin and Guitar Club entered this Mississippi Riverboat float in 1971.

Before Macclesfield's police force was taken over and amalgamated,
the town had its own Chief Constable. He was Henry Sheasby
pictured here in his dress uniform.

For many years the Bethel Band entertained countless Maxonians. They are pictured during the 1930s in South Park.

St Michael's Church Lads' Brigade around the turn of the century at the Parish Church. Back row centre is Bob Sumner RAMC Sergeant. Front row, left: the Rev. Squibbs. Next to him is Staff Sgt Louis Matthews. This photo was probably taken just after the church was restored. The brigade met twice a week in St Michael's Institute while the church was being restored.

Dad's Army: The Macclesfield Home Guard in a picture probably taken at the end of the World War II. The Home Guard headquarters was in one of the Twelve Apostles in Park Lane.

With colours flying, members of the Cheshire Regiment salute Macclesfield Home Guard on parade outside Cooksons in Waters Green after the war.

The year is 1913 and members of the Cheshire Regiment parade outside the Town Hall. The pending war was snapping at their heels and the horrors of the French campaign beckoned on the horizon.

October 2nd, 1929, and HRH Prince Henry the Duke of Gloucester arrives at Macclesfield Town Hall on the occasion of the opening of Trentabank Reservoir. Notice the Union Gateway to the left of the Town Hall.

National Fire Service Personnel who served during the second world war in Macclesfield. A young Eric Burgess, who had an engineering firm in Stanley Street from the 1950s onwards, is seen sixth from the left back row.

Macclesfield St John Ambulance Brigade personnel line up for inspection, date not known.

Officers and sergeants of the old Macclesfield 5th Volunteer Battalion Cheshire Regiment, based at The Barracks. Included are Sergeants Ernest and Walter Hackney, Lockyer, Taylor and Rushton.

Macclesfield Army Cadets at Pensarn Camp, 1944. Major Francis Bullock (just visible between cadets Graham Naden and Bernard Cox, top left) with Roy Booth, Ken Watson, Cadet Kershaw, Brian Roberts, Brian Cockayne, Geoff Moss, Reg Biggar, Geoff Hunter and others.

BWA Hurdsfield's fire brigade around the 1950s with the mill's tender.

Macclesfield Girl Guides during a 'sewing circle' making toys for charitable purposes.

Macclesfield Borough Police Force in the Market Place with WH Smith's in the background parading to the Parish Church as part of the Mayor's Sunday civic parade. The year is probably 1946.

Macclesfield Borough Police Force, pre 1950, line up for the camera at the rear of the Police Station at Town Hall.

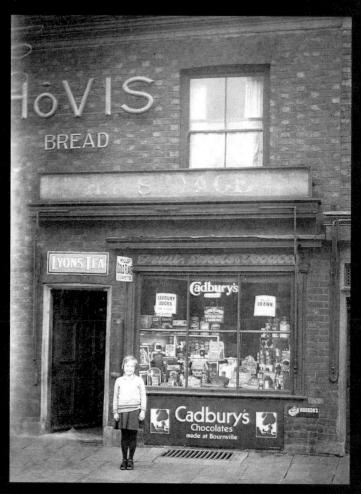

Joan Savage, later to become Joan Mottershead, outside her parents' shop in Buxton Road in 1933.

Pictured in the 1930s: Pimblott's bread and confectionery shop was situated on Mill Street between Stanley Street and Castle Street. Pimblott's was renowned for well-baked products; so much so that their premises were often referred to as 'The Burnt Offering' shop! The tea-room, upstairs, was frequently in demand following funerals when buttered currant bread was traditionally served. The adjacent boot and shoe shop was Kordians.

The lady in the picture is Mrs Hall, seen with her daughter, who gained her cap and gown for music and who married local builder Jack Marsden. The Old Mill Lane shop was on the corner of Poole Street and is now a chip shop.

Still going strong after many decades, J J Cookson's Central Motor Garage is pictured in the early 1930s at the corner of Albert Place and Waters Green.

A 1935 photograph of Frank Burgess's radio and bicycle shop in Sunderland Street on the corner of Pickford Street. Frank's beloved Triumph motor car, nicknamed 'Gloria' is seen parked to the side. Today this shop is part of the Blackshaw Bros (Merchants) premises.

Hillman and Humber cars, plus Austin Cambridge, were on offer at Gleave Motors, Davenport Street and Buxton Road (on the site of the old Royal Oak) when this 1960s' picture was taken. A chimney in the background has an advertisement on it saying: 'Cook, Builder and Contractor'.

Always a favourite: The Maypole Dairy Co Ltd's shop in Mill Street.

This photograph of Gleave Motors was taken in 1961.

To the left of the Swan wi' Two Necks (but when the picture was taken in the 1960s it had lost the abbreviation and was 'with' Two Necks) was Wellings Chemists. Greenall Whitley's King's Head was adjacent.

The Grate House: Montague Jones's shop in Samuel Street, where Macclesfield sills could be purchased, in the 1930s. To the right was Allen and Hudson's.

How many recollect Corbishley's electrical stores in Westminster Street off Chestergate? You may recall it was just next to the public toilets and here we have a glimpse inside this small electrical store in the 1950s. Corbishley's also had a public address system, a familiar site at many outdoor events.

The photo on the left, top, is of J. Forrest and Son, butchers, of 69 Chestergate (renowned for their sausages) taken in the late 1940s. The lack of beef and pork joints hanging from the rail seen in the upper half of the shop window is explained by the fact that rationing was still in vogue.

Above: Joe Forrest Junior is seen in the mid 1930s posing on one of the Sebastopol cannons and carriages in West Park.

Left: S. W. Morley's jewellers in the 1940s.

An extremely old print of Wainwright's, a shoemaker, leather cutter and clogger of Commercial Road.

An old shop in Windmill Street later to become Cundiff's but this was taken around the turn of the century.

The old Pack Horse in Jordangate now demolished. The bowling green at the rear was home to the famous Pack Horse Bowling Club for many a year.

Perkins Sweet Shop, Buxton Road.
(The Cinema is seen just to the left).

A tobacconist's shop in Jordangate, opposite Cumberland House, pictured in the 1930s. There was an entry by the side of the shop leading to a cottage where 'Tripe Joe' lived - so named because he bleached the tripe for the UCP Restaurant at 13 Chestergate.

Above: Jospeph Bagnall's shop in
Mill Lane as it was in May, 1937,
for the coronation of King George
V1 and Queen Elizabeth.

Above right: The Ring o' Bells in
King Edward Street. It later became
a frozen food establishment.

Mr Samuel Fox's corner shop at
62 The Waters, which faced
towards Sunderland Street and in
more recent times has been taken
over by The Old Mill Stone public
house next door. Mrs Fox and
Rosie the cook pose for this late
Edwardian picture.

Again, the Ring o' Bells: when the landlord was John Eccles (believed to be pictured far right) who moved to Chestergate where he had the charabanc business and public house.

The Baths Hotel, Green Street, Macclesfield. Thomas E.E. Beanlands was landlord when this picture was taken.

An errand boy, basket over his arm, strolls by the Old Mill Stone.

A lady, thought to be the landlady's daughter, poses outside the Black's Head Hotel, Mill Street.

This photo of the Nag's Head, occupying the corner at the bottom of the 108 Steps to this day. In 1859 the departing landlord was Richard Stubbs and Jonathan Heald took over (his name can be seen over the door). In 1875 when Heald was 70 years of age the Nags Head was sold to John Sheldon for £1,225. This photograph could well date from 1872 when the Central Station was opened and there was a great deal of activity in the area.

A close-up of the Old Sun Inn at the Town Hall end of Chestergate close to where the Natwest Bank now is. This photo dates from circa 1880.

One of the smallest beerhouses in Macclesfield was at the corner of Ryle Street and Hobson Street. The last landlord was William Farrer.

An extremely old view of The Cock Inn, Henbury.

Thomas Pickford's White Lion brewery in Duke Street/Mill Street. In the early part of the twentieth century the brewery was still going strong, the beer being sold in the pub. The buildings to the left of the public house have now been demolished.

Park Green Brewery in 1970, just as it was being demolished. Lonsdale and Adshead's brewery sold to Ind Coope. The steps leading to the firm's offices had been demolished by the time this picture was taken. To the right can be seen Mellor's paper shop and Les Shingles'.

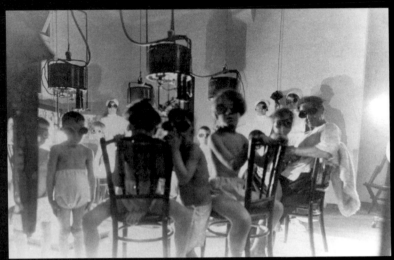

Macclesfield children taking part in artifical sunlight treatment at Macclesfield Infirmary in 1925. It was, presumably, to help with a cure for rickets.

This little lad is strapped to the chair as he receives treatment for his eyes at the Infirmary in the 1920s.

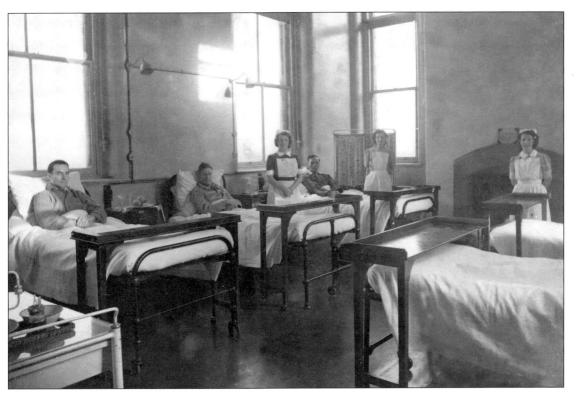

The men's ward at West Park in the late 1940s.

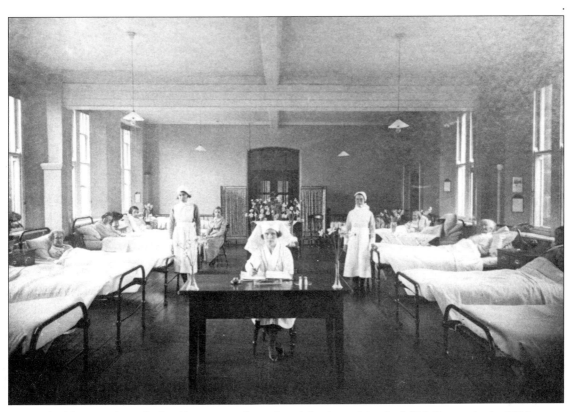

Pristine bedsheets and starched uniforms were the order of the day at Macclesfield Infirmary in the 1930s.

Plenty of flowers in a Macclesfield female ward.

Christmas decorations by the score. This postcard says it was sold, price 3d, in aid of Macclesfield Infirmary in 1922.

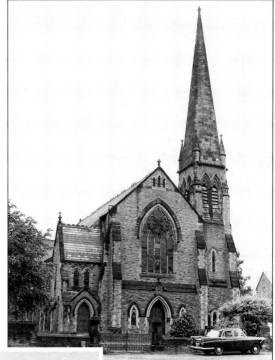

Top left: King Edward Street Unitarian Chapel, little changed over the years.

Top right: Trinity Church, Cumberland Street, demolished in the late 1960s.

Above: Broken Cross Wesleyan Sunday School. This postcard was addressed to my great aunt, Annie Bowyer, at 48 Broken Cross, in 1910.

Right: Brunswick Chapel, Brunswick Street, Macclesfield.

This faded photograph of the Daybrook Street entrance to Victoria Park taken before the war showing the park lodge where Mr and Mrs Blakelow lived in those times. The gates and railings were sacrificed for the 1939-45 war effort. These stone pillars are still in place but the balls on top have been lost to vandalism.

Victoria Park in its heyday.

Macclesfield's market cross, the stocks, stones from Macclesfield Castle and the stone from the top of one of Macclesfield's wells, all congregated in West Park before they were removed.

Victoria Park's delightful Avenue.

Another ancient photograph of The Avenue in Victoria Park.

West Park bandstand in 1932. Many Maxonians pause to listen to the band, probably on a Sunday afternoon.

This 'doll's house' park keeper's lodge, long an attraction for visitors.

South Park Pavilion, Macclesfield, burnt down and now re-built.

South Park's tennis courts in use during the 1930s.

Another look at South Park's tennis courts as spectators watch the sport in the 1930s.

Sunderland Street, Macclesfield, with the Central Station in the background. The 'Thanks to the Donor' arch and banner refer to the opening of Victoria Park.

An old tyme music hall at St Peter's Memorial Hall, circa 1953. Left to right: Mrs C. Brown, Miss Perrin, May Hillman, Helen Varty (piano), Mrs Jackson, Phyllis Green, Alice Till and Ethel Brindley.

A circa 1967 photograph of St Alban's headmaster Mr Noden and his wife celebrating the 21st birthday of son John.

Photographer J. Albinson did not need to carry his camera and tripod far to capture this evocative 1930 picture outside The Majestic Cinema, for his studio was just around the corner in Roe Street. The occasion was a farewell to The Majestic's manager Mr Vic Ollerenshaw seen on the steps, centre of entrance, who was leaving to be area manager of several Manchester-based cinemas. The date was Saturday October 25 and the time about 8.20pm. Seat prices were 6d, 9d, 1/- and 1/6 for adults and 2d, 4d, 6d and 9p (balcony) for children.

The 7th Macclesfield (Brunswick) Scout Group's Gang Show 1966. On the photograph is Billy Richardson the Scoutmaster and a young Michael Baron and Ian Storer. Brunswick were formed in 1909 and continued until the Chapel was closed. Billy joined the group around 1920 and became one of the longest-serving leaders in the district.

In this 1968 picture Frankie Woods entertains the children at KEK Christmas party for employees' youngsters and children from the School for the Deaf at Cheadle.

The Co-op Field Treat, Ecton Avenue, about 1947. There are many young faces here who are now grandparents in the town.

Inside the 'Tin Tab', or St Michael's Parochial Church Hall in the 1930s, which burnt down in the 1970s. Note the gas mantle, centre. The occasion is thought to be a sale of work or fayre.

The venue is thought to be the Morton Hall, Union Road. Mr Harry Pleath of Bollington is seen in his fireman's uniform centre back. Amelia Alice Kent is centre, wearing white. Alf Flood is on the right. His wife is sitting in front of Mrs Kent. They used to lead off a lot of dances in the early 1950s.

The Dormel Singers, conductor Dorothy Mellor and pianist Len Lea, pictured in July 1952.

John Mills, now Sir John, and Patricia Roc pictured beneath Goyt Bridge (now flooded) during the filming of 'So Well Remembered' in Macclesfield and district shortly after the World War II. Later, a charity showing in the early 1980s at The Majestic resulted in a full house. It was organised by Keith Yearsley, Peter Higginbotham and Doug Pickford. Here is the letter Sir John sent to Doug Pickford.

I am very sorry not to be able to be with you tonight, but I am recording a new play for the BBC. I am particularly disappointed as I so very well remember the filming in Macclesfield.

I shall never forget the day when, playing a local MP, I made an impassioned speech in the Market Place. The cameras were hidden on the roof and many people rushed up to me after I had finished and, with tears in their eyes, swore they would vote for me because I was offering them exactly what they wanted! I was really quite at a loss for words!

I do hope you all enjoy the film and I hope to visit Macclesfield again before long.

Sir John Mills, CBE

The front of The Opera House, Catherine Street. This and the next are rare pictures indeed. The theatre was destroyed by fire on April 4, 1931. Curiously enough, the site of the theatre has never been built upon and today serves as a car park between 16 Catherine Street and Oasis Florist. (John Patterson).

The Foyer, Opera House, Catherine Street (see companion photo).

Rose Marie at The Majestic in 1949. Jean Patterson is front right. Jean went on to have her own highly successful dancing school, and starred in productions at the Majestic for many years.

The year is 1948, war is over, and it is time to be happy again.

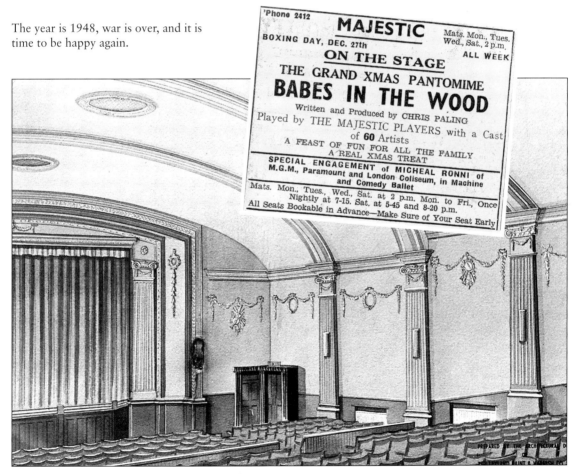

'Phone 2412 **MAJESTIC** Mats. Mon., Tues. Wed., Sat., 2 p.m.

BOXING DAY, DEC. 27th ALL WEEK

ON THE STAGE

THE GRAND XMAS PANTOMIME

BABES IN THE WOOD

Written and Produced by CHRIS PALING

Played by THE MAJESTIC PLAYERS with a Cast of **60** Artists

A FEAST OF FUN FOR ALL THE FAMILY

A REAL XMAS TREAT

SPECIAL ENGAGEMENT of MICHEAL RONNI of M.G.M., Paramount and London Coliseum, in Machine and Comedy Ballet

Mats. Mon., Tues., Wed., Sat. at 2 p.m. Mon. to Fri., Once Nightly at 7-15. Sat. at 5-45 and 8-20 p.m.

All Seats Bookable in Advance—Make Sure of Your Seat Early

The interior of The Majestic, now demolished.

Members of Macclesfield Rotary Club just after World War II in a picture that is presumed to be a 'pig club' where groups of people would pool their money to buy a pig for much-needed meat. Pictured are Frank Hooley, Eric Kite, Arthur Collins, Adam McVey, Ron Groves, Stan Hunter, Cyril Lloyd, Harry Massey.

A social gathering at St James' School, Sutton, about 1949. Mr and Mrs Arthur Kelly and daughter Rita are among those on the left of the picture. George Foot and Raymond Heapy are also included in the company.

Halle Mill's Christmas dance, circa 1948. Master of ceremonies Norman Mitchell (with pail) appears to have everything under control!

A social gathering at the Stanley Hall, Macclesfield. Many dances and other functions were held at the Stanley Hall until its demolition in the late 1960s.

The Beehive Restaurant (owned by the Co-op) in Sunderland Street was a popular venue for decades. It was also the scene for many meetings. The Rotary Club of Macclesfield, not to mention the Inner Wheel and many other societies, used this as their base.

A rose queen parade at Victoria Park. Elsie Weaver is on the extreme right and the lady in the hat, left, is Miss Kirkham.

Gawsworth Rose Queen, 1976. Top row, left to right: Vivien Potts, Fensome twins, Rose Queen Paula Wheelton, Joan Davenport, Amanda Belfield, Jane Harrop. Row two: Alison Moffit, Jackie Birch. Row 3: Kate Wilbraham, Sarah Hayes, Sharn Willock, Debbie Willock, Kate Harding, Susan Wainwirght, Suzanne Searles, Carol Tuck. Bottom row: Angela Wheelton, Rhiannon Jones, Sandra Tuck, ? Bolton, Lorraine Higgins, Claire Webb, Maria Stevens, Susan Lee.

Stamford Road Methodist Church's first Rose Queen Julie Perry, in 1963. Back row: John Green, Percy Naden, Mrs Connie Palin. Attendants were Carol and Jackie Longden, Barbara McKie, Susan Holmes, Karen Bould, Judith Holmes, Keith Goodier, Nigel Homes.

You can almost smell the liniment and embrocation! Lining up with the hard casey football, their polished football boots complete with nailed-in studs, Brocklehurst Whiston's team of the 1929-30 season display three trophies - cause for celebration indeed.

These smart young gentlemen were the Townley Street Sunday School football team of 1910-11. Notice the jaunty way the chap on the front row, second from right, wears a scarf.

Athey Street School football team of 1933-34. The lads have won a fine trophy and line up for the photographer in the boys' playground.

Northern Athletic, 1953/4. Back row, left to right: G. Hewitt, G. Crowder, P. Jones, F. Roberts, B. Wilson, G. Batten, F. Corners, F. Stoneley, W. Crowder (manager). Front, left to right: K. Simpson, J. Wood, F. Lawson, P. Barnett, J. Cooper.

St John's Church in the background was demolished and re-built on The Weston, only to be demolished again. Here, the Cheshire Shield footballing heroes of the church line up after the 1928-29 season.

The venue is West Park, the era is the late 1920s and the occasion is a line-up of gentlemen bowlers. The trophy in the centre may well be the Times Trophy, played for annually.

A sporting group from Byron Street School, about 1929, winners of the school's sports held on Moss Rose football ground.

An interesting item of Macclesfield sporting history. The Macclesfield Schoolboys team pictured in this 1932-3 football season is the only one ever to win the Cheshire County Schoolboy Shield, achieved at Wallasey. Arthur Shufflebotham was captain and is seen holding the trophy. The goalkeeper, third from left, back row, was Gerry Potter who later became managing director of Brocklehurst Whiston. To the right of him are Harold Norbury, Fred Walton and young Craven. Doug Parr is extreme left, front row.

Smiling faces at a dinner of the Macclesfield and District Referees' Association, some time in the 1950s.

A 1977 photograph showing some well-known characters of Macclesfield table tennis life, and their wives, posing for the camera in the Masonic Hall before dinner is served to celebrate the association's 50 years of existence. Included are John Hedley Palin and Ernie Hackney.

A group of Macclesfield table tennis enthusiasts pose for the camera about 1958. Standing, left to right: G. Hunter, T. Hunter, J. Perry, B. Hough, — , P. Jones, N. Hodson, R. Hodkinson, G. Higginbotham, B. Crain, J. McKimmie, A. Jones, E. Hulse, P. Rhodes. Seated: G. Cunningham, R. Wilkinson, M. McKimmie, B. Booth.

A Macclesfield Boxing Club photo taken in the clubroom at the Joiners Arms in Paradise Street in 1946. Back row, left to right: Harry Greenwood, Jackie Stubbs, Jack Gill, Joey Dixon, Philip Johnson, Everard Allen. Front row: Graham Till, Don Harper, Eric Gosling, Ralph Greenwood, —, —, Geoff Scragg. Eric Gosling said: 'Sadly, we had to find a new clubroom. What with skipping, sparring, etc., the plaster on the ceiling above the bar started to flake off, dropping into the customers' drinks. Oh, happy days!'

Macclesfield Baths in Davenport Street was a well-used place over the years, with separate sessions for men and women. One of the stalwarts of the swimming scene in town during the 1930s was Fred Bramhall, who won many competitions. Pictured with him in 1936, complete with trophies, are brothers Philip and Maurice Mottershead.

Wearing the Macclesfield coat of arms on their chests, these members of the Macclesfield Rugby Club pose for the camera in 1928.

'Hookie' Francis, science master at the Central School, is pictured (left) with the winners of the Crew Cup in 1935.

A 1930s walking race starting from outside Young's Builders Yard in Westminster Street, Macclesfield. The policeman in the centre is the well-known P.C. Norbury, affectionately known as 'Big Alec'.

St. Alban's football team, 1947. Back row, left to right: Frank Lewis, Fred Mannion, Charlie Oliver, Ken Grice, Ron Few, Bob Hewitt, Bryn Whitehurst, Fred Roberts, Harry Frodsham. Front: Arthur Duffy, John Moores, Hubert Jordan, Ricky Jones, Owen Mulrooney.

Stamford Road Methodist Church's first table tennis team in the 1951-52 season. Back row, left to right: Neville Grant, R.L. (Skip) Rogers, Colin Bowers, Ted Wigley. Front: Tom Capper, Roy Thompson, Bert Capper, Ken Farrar. In their inaugural year this team had to play all home matches at Lord Street Sunday School.

Left: Sutton walkers and supporters seen at Gawsworth in 1947. Third from the left is Mr Frank Yates Snr., a prolific walker early in the century, and on the far right is Macclesfield industrialist Mr Edmund Lomas.

Right: Mr Frank Bowyer, manager of Macclesfield Town FC, presents the 10-mile trophy to Sutton Walking Club's Don Warren, circa 1962. Others shown at this Church House Inn presentation include Messrs Francis Bullock, Ernie Twigg, Eric Oldfield and Dick Barnard, Snr.

Left: Sutton Walking Club's Don Warren is shown breasting the tape and the record in the 1950 Cheshire Championship two mile event – a title he retained for an astonishing 21 years!

A Macclesfield Harriers Group photographed at London Road Sunday School (their regular changing venue) in 1948-9. Standing, left to right: Mr Welch (Treasurer), J. Moores, Selwyn Walton, Joe Smith, Arthur Evans, Jack Lee, Mike Lafferty, — , Fred Culley, Dennis Clayton, Derek Sims, Frank Gratton, Geoff Hunter, Stan Cook. Front: Peter Dunlop, Graham Wright, Joe Vare, —, —.

A Macclesfield Harriers' group, circa 1950, taken outside Sutton Ex-Servicemen's Club. Standing, left to right: Mr Welch, Treasurer, Albert Rigby, Arthur Evans, Jack Lee, Joe Smith, John Norton. Front: Stan Cook, Derek Sims, Jim Mottershead, Geoff Hunter, Fred Culley.

Windsmoor's football club, 1951. Many mills and factories had their own teams, many of which entered the Macclesfield Workshops competition. Back row, left to right: Johnny Davis, Philip Barnet, —, Tommy Lawson, Andy Ames, Cyril Gosling, Derek Massey, Abe Boswell. Front: Jimmy McKie, T. Scott, Hubert Jordan, Owen Mulrooney, Danny Deery.

This photograph of Wm Frost's Workshops Knockout team dates from about 1937. This annual competition, held on Puss Bank, off Buxton Road, took place over the Easter break each year. Young Jack Cross from the Pet Shop, Waters Green, is the player seen extreme left, front row. Subsequently, Jack devoted his entire working life to Frost's as an engineer, taking leave only to serve his country as a Royal Engineer throughout World War II.

An early 1960s BWA football team. Back row, left to right: Harry Mottram, Jim Ratcliffe, Derek Oldham, Alan Littler, Paul Mannion, Mo Swindells, Eric Siddons, John Bailey. Front: Brian Rushton, Harold Goodwin, Herbert Percival, Peter Robinson, David Holland, John Abbott.

This is understood to be of Macclesfield Boys' Club table tennis competitors, taken in the late 1950s. The gentleman seated in the centre, with glasses, is the late T.H.(Harry) Hayes, who was editor of the Macclesfield Courier and, later, editor of the Macclesfield Advertiser which was at 54 Chestergate.

The infant class at Crompton Road School in 1893. The pupil second from the right at the back is Louis H. Matthews, then about seven. His daughter has provided a number of photos for this book.

Miss Clayton's sewing class at Byron Street School, probably early twentieth century.

There are a lot of Macclesfield people on this 1928 Gawsworth School picture. William P. Blench, who went on to be a Metropolitan policeman, Guardsman, teacher at Bollington Cross Primary School and, in later years, an employee of the Cheshire Building Society, is pictured centre back.

St Andrew's School around 1913. Miss Gladys Moseley is on the left.

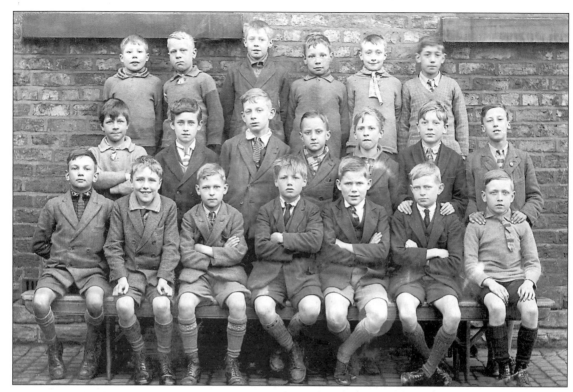

St George's School, 1930.

St Paul's School about 1944. The teachers were Miss Topham and Mr Brown the headmaster. Back row: — , Geoffrey Challinor, Barry Wood, — , Norman Clayton, Keith Barnett, Barry Nelson, David Connor. Middle row: — , Ken Potts, — , — , Geoffrey Rowley, — ,— , David Watling. Front row: Anne Slater, Edna Jeffries, Margaret Rowson, Pat Belton, Janet Carter, Doreen Hannigan, Jean Gibbons, Sheila Tristram, Brenda Ratcliffe.

The unveiling of the new King's School gates of remembrance in 1949 by His Grace the Duke of Westminster.

A class of Macclesfield High School for Girls, May, 1923.

Hurdsfield Boys' School soccer team of 1953 posed for this picture in Daybrook Street schoolyard. Back row, left to right: Mr N. Tattersall, Arthur Bullock, John Heath, Dennis Brown, John Hammond, ? Clarke. Middle: Terry Beech, Ken Curley, Barry Hillman, Reg Berrisford, Ken Houghton. Front: Dave Swanson, —.

Byron Street Junior School, approximately 1943. Miss E. Ingham (with dog, Laddie) was head mistress. The teacher was Derek Worrel. There is another photograph with Miss Ingham and Laddie further on.

St Paul's School, Glegg Street, Macclesfield, 1946. Back row, left to right: Miss Joan Brooks, John Watling, James Whittaker, Bert Cotterill, Phil Green, Graham Bridge, Geoff Amos, Denis Heapy, Alan Holmes, Ken Osborne, Mr Brown (headmaster). Middle: Mary Barnett, Michael Forrest, Alan Smith, — , Alan Eves, Graham Arthur, Brian Jolley, Paul Gaskell, Brian Davenport, — . Front: Helen Adshead, Brenda Ratcliffe, Helen Murray, Valerie Bowers, Violet Wyatt, Kathlenn — , Shirley Smith, Eileen Bowler, Mary Lea, Alice Millar, Sylvia Corbishley. Teacher Miss Brooks married Cllr. Gordon Landon who was elected to be Mayor of Macclesfield, but died before attaining office. Mrs Landon eventually emigrated to Australia.

Christ Church School of 1959.

The same class at a later school photograph.

Early school years of the twentieth century featured the British Empire to a great extent. Macclesfield pupil Willie Kidd was one among millions of schoolchildren of the British Empire who, in 1915, helped bring happiness on Christmas Day to the armed forces.

Empire Day was always a time for celebration and, the following year, young Willie was presented with this certificate (bottom).

Macclesfield Central Secondary School for Boys, 1949, academic and sporting award recipients. The back row includes the following: Michael Corcoran, Brian Marsden, Bernard Tebay, Brian Holland, Philip Parr, Philip Broadhead and Philip Oldham. Middle: Mick Baguley, Terry Wesley, ? Beech, Denis Heapy (head prefect), David McGuinness and Ken Sweetmore. Front row: Colin Holloway, Gerald Nixon, Brian Cox, Barry Harding, Alan Brown, Graham Bramwell, Gordon Harrison and Jim Howard. These youngsters proved to be a hugely successful group in later life. Mike Corcoran, Terry Wesley and Colin Holloway excelled in sport, for example, and many others succeeded in business; not least Brian Cox who progressed to become Director of Finance at Warwick District Council. David McGuiness, a former teacher at Upton Priory Junior School, is now a popular stage entertainer.

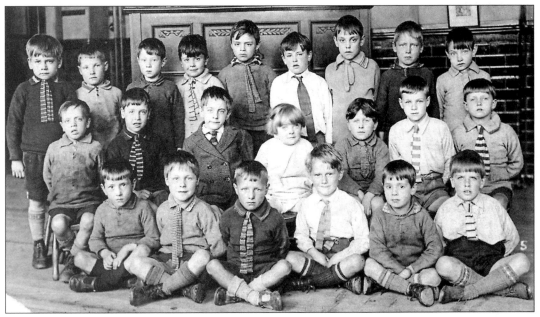

Athey Street School, 1930. Back row from left: John Sutton, David Gosling, Bob Weston, Graham Higginbotham, Bernard Fitter, Roy Barker, John Leech, Ernie Lawrenson, Phillip Potts. Middle: Frank Bailey, Harold Malbourn, Wallace Ledgar, W. Ledgar's younger brother, Norman Howarth, Dennis Ridgway, John Wetton. Front row from left: Herbert Burgoyne, John Cook, Ken Raybould, Harry Braid, Maurice Winnell, Ken Dunkey.

Byron Street School, 1951-2. Back row, left to right: P. Slack, D. Scott, K. Hooley, D. Keogh, M. Mellor, R. Rigby, P. Slater, D. Rushton, C. Sumner, Miss B.M. Skellern (deputy head). Second row: M. Bailey, D. Stacey, M. Simpson, R. Bailey, C. White, D. Burgess, J. Spearing, T. Barton. Third row: S. Broadhurst, C. Lear, R. Johnson, P. Hulley, Miss E. Ingham, head (with Laddie), J. Capper, R. Wren, M. Goodwin, I. Poynton. Fourth row: J. Brocklehurst, R. Barton, C. Proudlove, —, T. Weston, M. Hancocks, R. Hodkinson, R. Wrench. Front row: V. Johnson, K. Oliver, I. Bailey, C. Jones, J. Newton, M. Greaves.

Byron Street School, 1933. Back row: Marion Dickson, —, Jean Shaw, Rene Thompson, Sylvia Steele, Brenda Clowes, Mary Earlam, ? Foster. Centre row: Joan Burgess, Margaret Oliver, Betty Wilkinson, Shelagh Hill, Florence Wright, Marion Johnson. Front row: —, Irene Powell, Margaret Davenport, Irene Knutton, Beryl Broadhurst, Betty Taylor, Joyce Smith.

Byron Street School, about 1929. Names offered are: Daisy Unsworth, Eric Lockett, Margaret Larsen, Dennis Heath, Douglas Allen, Arthur Biddulph, Fred Nield, Vernon Lovatt, Philip Dale, Bill Thornley, Clifford Hill, Colin Blackshaw, Dorothy Torey, Hilda Mottershead, Joyce Potts, Irene Hardy, Phyllis Mitchell, Vera Hardy, Kenneth Knox, Joyce Gould, Hilda Bates, Irene Kennerley, Dorothy Nisbett, Hilda Belfield, Philip Belfield.

Byron Street School, 1926-27. Top: Bill Leonard, Charlie Parker, Sam Cresswell, Philip Moores, — , Freddy Craven, Arthur Massey, Charlie Lightfoot, Ray Kirk. Middle: Jim Walker, — , John Jackson, Ken Lovatt, Bill Holland, Freddie Lewis, — , George Neil, Arthur Davis. Front: Bill Vernon, Ken Brough, Bill Thornley, Eric Burgess, — , Tom Herrity, Frank Talks, Colin Blackshaw, —. All the boys have small models, and it is therefore presumed to be the model-making class.

Athey Street School circa 1924. Some names are: Herbert Walley, — Malkin, Harold Edge, Harry Chadwick, Arthur Elkin, Harold Berrisford, Syd Barlow, Wilf Upton, Syd Poynton.

St George's School in May, 1925. Back row: Marjorie Clews, Muriel Shatwell, Connie Downing, Audrey Jepson, Roy Robinson, Dorothy Wood, Edna Hardgreaves, Lena Cooney. Middle: A. Scragg, Katie Steer, Hilda Bosson, Irene Wrigley, Ivy Brocklehurst. Front: Dorothy Harrop, Dorothy Bennett, Barbara — , Alice — .

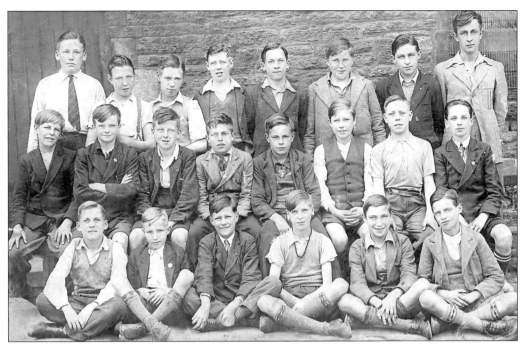

Hurdsfield Boys' School, 1939, just before the onset of the second world war. Back row: Alfred Mellor, Ken Grice, Jim Walley, Harold Genders, Ken Arnold, Arthur Cottrell, Colin Hamson, Robin Wood. Second: Ivan Haywood, Roy Hall, Alec Robertson, Tom Sutton, Erix Stevenson, Norman Grainger, Albert Sheratt, — ?. Front: Leslie Mathers, Derek Roberts, Wilf Woodward, Derick Wild, Gordon Cobbam, Raymond Bradley.

This superb photograph of Trinity Square School teachers and pupils in 1928-9 includes the following names: Miss Miriam Swindells, Margaret Hadfield, Maude Hill, Mary Frost, Olive Clowes, Miss Malburn, Barbara Greenall, Lily Houghton, Nellie Brooks, Florence Penny, Joan Garner, Eileen Hunter, Constance Macdonald, Joyce Walker, Lilian McCarthy, Eileen Pownall, Alice Swindells, Lily Potts, Marjorie Bailey, Phyllis Burns, Constance Vare, Christina Brown.

St George's School in 1906. The head master was Mr Salt.

St Paul's School, 1926-7. Back row: Marcella Stubbs, Annie Coates, Vera Jones, Peggy Wilson, Ada Broadhurst. Second: Hilda Ford, Olive Davies, Abigail Cobham, Irene Cooper, Mabel Harrison. Third: — , Annie Barnet, Winifred Cross, Joan Devine, Lily Wyatt, Eleanor Frisk. Fourth: Eva Hadfield, Louise Hackney, Wilfred Cobham, Amy Beard, Mildred Beard, Peggy Osborne. Front: Irene Hadsfield, — , Joan Bailey, Margaret Sherratt, Elsie Buckley.

Duke Street School of 1935. Margaret Watson (later Mrs Margaret Brooks) is second from the right, back row. Others named are: Gwyneth Orme, Nellie Woods and Joyce Etchells.

Mill Street School has now been demolished to make way for a supermarket and was, in point of fact, not in Mill Street! It was between Pickford Street and Lower Exchange Street in the area once known as Pudding Bag Street. Here, some young lady pupils in the girls' playground observe the solar eclipse in 1929.

This photograph of a class at Ash Grove School, believed to have been taken about 1955 shows headmaster Mr Lea and teacher Mrs Bendilow with, among other pupils, Melvyn Perry, Stewart Bailey, Ann Cotterill, Tony Wardle, John Hayes, Michael Clarke, Paul Howarth and Paul Carroll.

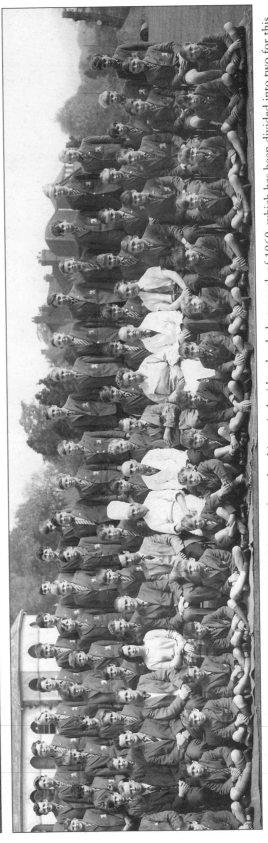

The entire Beech Hall Preparatory School, Macclesfield, turned out for this typical wide school photograph of 1960, which has been divided into two for this book. Notice that even the chefs appeared on the photograph.

Pupils of Wincle Primary School before a trip to Belle Vue Zoo, Manchester, around 1950.

The bridge at Swan Pool, Macclesfield, at the top of Buxton Road.

The main road through Bollington. The words on the back, sent to a Mrs Walker of Stockport in 1905, say: 'Dear Mother, They did not seem to have any other views of Bollington only what I have sent before besides this one. Hoping you will like it. Best love to all from Harry and myself.'

Henshall Road, Bollington Cross, with Bollington Cross school on the left.

This postcard view of the Cock and Pheasant at Broken Cross was sent about 1900 from well-known Bollington footballer Tommy Nolan to Lizzie Bamford.

Many will recall The Market Square in Bollington. Here, four local chaps have a bit of fun posing for the camera whilst in the stocks, which were a feature there for many years.

We have seen Bollington's stocks. Now it is time for Rainow's. This was taken in the 1930s and shows Frank Evans (who was 74 in 1990 when this shot was supplied to me, and was then living in Llandudno).

The walk down across the river to the Recreation Ground, Bollington.

Nylon sizing (gumming) at Olivers Mill, Bollington in the early 1960s.

A pre-war procession, photographed from The Aqueduct, goes past the Memorial Gardens, Bollington. Was it a carnival?

Satan, Hitler's biggest 4,000lb bomb, receives some coppers from a Bollington schoolboy, thought to be John Plant, who needs steps to allow him to reach the money hole.

It is the World War II and three German bombs, thankfully not dangerous any more, are used to collect money for the war effort, outside the Council Offices.

For countless years, White Nancy, astride Kerridge Hill, has been a favourite haunt for picnics, and also for camping, as this 1940s picture shows.

Pott Shrigley in the 1920s, with the church gates on the left and the school on the right.

Another 1920s view of Pott Shrigley, with the church on the right.

Martha Harding and daughter Beryl on the steps of the village shop, Pott Shrigley, in June, 1928.

An Edwardian photograph of Pott Shrigley. St Christopher's church and the row of cottages have changed but little.

H. Ottley, saddler, in Wellington Road, Bollington. It looks as though he sold much more, including oils and garden equipment.

An idyllic Monks Heath scene before traffic lights and the motor car.

Old thatched cottages at Monk's Heath, or Monkseath as it says on this postcard.

The ancient cross at Gawsworth at the turn of the century. Its well-worn steps are testament to how well it has been used, either for worship or as a market cross, over the centuries. This photograph was taken around 1902.

The postmark on the postcard says 1907 but the photograph was probably taken a few years prior to that. Notice that the main road by Poynton Church is not tarmaced.

Langley Band parades from the Methodist Church down Main Road in the late 1920s.

Some familiar faces here in this Langley photograph of 1923. Back row: Cyril Dawson, H. Downes, H. Manifold. Front: Mark Fernyhough, R. Noble, R. Dawson, R. Meakin.

Langley Fire Brigade pose in front of Langley Hall for this 1921 photograph. Back row, left to right (aboard vehicle): Harry Tideswell, Tom Cumberledge, George Priestnall, Harry Dawson (captain), Fred Kite, Joe Oldham, Fred Lomas. Standing in front: Bill Hambleton, Wilf Hulley, Tom Barton, Gilbert Warren, Bill Warren.

The village of Langley suitably bedecked for a celebration in the early part of the century. It may have been for the ending of hostilities in World War I.

A pony and trap pose for the cameraman outside the Church House, Higher Sutton, about 1929.

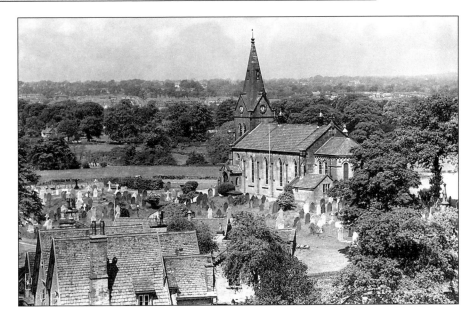

The church of St James, Sutton, taken in the 1950s.

The famous, or infamous, winter of 1947, when heavy snow laid siege to the area for many weeks. This was the scene at Leek Road, Bosley.

Another view of the heavy snow at Leek Road, Bosley, in March, 1947.

The ancient and annual rushbearing ceremony at Forest Chapel, Macclesfield Forest. The ceremony of bringing rushes to the church and bedecking the interior dates back into the mists of time. It is held annually during August each year. This captivating photograph was taken during the very early part of the twentieth century.

Mathew Beethan was the landlord when this photograph of the Cat and Fiddle on the road to Buxton was taken. Notice the exterior shutters. There were also venetian blinds and curtains to the windows, not to mention interior shutters. This was obviously way before central heating!

A very different Rainow to the one today. This is, or was, Rainow before the new houses were built.

Another view of Rainow, this postcard scene being taken in the 1940s.

Three magnificent shire horses at Gurnett Smithy, Sutton. The Old King's Head is to the left.

The cart says Sutton Brewery, Macclesfield, and the sign says Stancliffe Ales. The scene is The Highwayman at Rainow about 1903.

Tom Steele, for many years the larger-than-life landlord of the Hanging Gate at Higher Sutton. He had only one arm, his right, and on the stump of his left there was a hook. The limb was shot off in a shotgun accident. This photo was taken of him behind the bar in the 1950s.

The Hanging Gate during the 1960s.

We have already seen photographs of Sutton Walking Club's athletes. Here some of the members and supporters pose cheerfully outside the Church House Inn about 1953, an event graced by Macclesfield's Mayor, Cllr J.B. Hidderley and the Mayoress.

A painting of 1928 by R.C. Riseley showing the site of Trentabank Reservoir before the vast undertaking was commenced.

Trentabank Reservoir under construction. When completed, in the late 1920s, the scheme provided a further 465,000 gallons of water daily for the thirsty town of Macclesfield, this increasing the daily supply per head of population from eight to 21.3 gallons.

Workmen constructing the reservoir. Some came from Manchester and Yorkshire, and a number stayed on in the district.

Some 40 plus years after its construction, this picture shows the reservoir during the drought of 1976.

Bosley Station, before Dr Beeching wielded his infamous axe in the 1960s.

Another picture of the accident scene. The lorry must have been travelling at a fair speed!